# Church and Synagogue
# Library Resources

## A CSLA Bibliography

### (Fourth Edition)

*Compiled by*

**Rachel Kohl and Dorothy Rodda**

A Church and Synagogue Library Association Publication
P.O. Box 1130, Bryn Mawr, PA  19010

# ABOUT THE COMPILERS

Rachel Kohl is librarian, St. Paul's United Methodist Church, Wilmington, Delaware and former chairman of the library services committee of the Church and Synagogue Library Association. Currently a public librarian, she was formerly a medical records librarian.

Dorothy Rodda is Executive Secretary of the Church and Synagogue Library Association. She received a master's degree in library science from Drexel University in Philadelphia and was librarian at the Ardmore (PA) Presbyterian Church. Formerly, she was a school and junior college librarian.

**Library of Congress Cataloging in Publication Data**

Kohl, Rachel.
  Church and synagogue library resources.

  A revised and updated ed. of Bibliography of church and synagogue library resources, edited by A.W. Swartout.
  1. Libraries, Church — Bibliography. 2. Synagogue libraries — Bibliography. I. Rodda, Dorothy, joint author. II. Swarthout, Arthur W. Bibliography of church and synagogue library resources. III. Title. IV. Series: Church and Synagogue Library Association. CSLA guide; no. 1.

Z675.C5K64   1975          016.0276'7          75-1178


**ISBN 0-915324-08-3**
(C) copyright 1975, Church and Synagogue Library Association.
Printed in the United States of America.
2nd edition 1975; 3rd edition 1979; 4th edition 1984.

# CONTENTS

# PREFACE

CHURCH AND SYNAGOGUE LIBRARY RESOURCES, fourth edition, was originally CSLA Guide No. 1. It has now been revised and updated as a CSLA bibliography for the third time. Like the three previous editions, it is intended to provide a basic list of the resources currently available to help librarians and library committees in organizing and operating effective church and synagogue libraries.

This bibliography has been compiled by Rachel Kohl and Dorothy Rodda under the sponsorship of the publications committee of the Church and Synagogue Library Association. The compilers especially wish to acknowledge the helpful suggestions of Jacqulyn Anderson, Church Library Department, Southern Baptist Convention; John Corrigan, CFX, Catholic Library Association; Nancy Dick, Evangelical Church Library Association; Ruth Frank, JWB Jewish Book Council; William Gentz, Claudia Hannaford, Margaret Korty, Evelyn Ling, Sally-Bruce McClatchey and Ruth Sawyer, all of the Church and Synagogue Library Association.

# 1. GENERAL AIDS

Barber, Cyril J. THE MINISTER'S LIBRARY. Baker, 1973. $17.95; vol 2. 1983. $14.95.
Vol. 1, Part I gives detailed directions for organizing a minister's library. Part II is a guide for choosing books in eleven categories. Vol. 2 includes books published 1972–1980.

Berhard, Genore H. HOW TO ORGANIZE AND OPERATE A SMALL LIBRARY. Highsmith, 1976. $3.
Step by step guidance for libraries without the services of a trained librarian.

BOOKER'S QUEST. Sound slide set. Evangelical Church Library Association, 1976. 80 color slides. 11 minute cassette tape. $35. Rental fee, $6. Rental fee, $6.
Booker T. Worm searches for the ideal church library.

BOWKER ANNUAL OF LIBRARY AND BOOK TRADE INFORMATION. $45.
Contains articles, statistics, lists of award-winning and best-selling books, lists of basic books and periodicals for librarians. Includes a library purchasing guide which lists library supplies and where you can buy them. Available in public libraries.

CHURCH AND SYNAGOGUE LIBRARIANSHIP.
A correspondence study course offered by The Center for Independent Study and Development, Division of Continuing Education, University of Utah. $50 plus $15.75 for required texts. Instructor: Ruth Sawyer. For information, write to CSLA or University of Utah, Correspondence Study, Division of Continuing Education, 1152 Annex Building, Salt Lake City, UT 84112.

THE CHURCH LIBRARY. A correspondence study course offered by Philadelphia College of Bible. $20. Instructor: Dorothy Black. For information, write: Correspondence School, Philadelphia College of Bible, Langhorne Manor, Langhorne, PA 19047.

THE CHURCH MEDIA CENTER. Filmstrip. Broadman, $18. 54 color frames, with manual and recording.
How to share information and promote understanding of the potential in the media center.

Ezell, Mancil. A CHURCH MEDIA LIBRARY AT WORK. Convention, 1984. $2.50.
Basic concept book not only for church library workers but also for church leaders and teachers. Gives information about media library purposes, personnel, financing, space and services.

Gates, Jean K. INTRODUCTION TO LIBRARIANSHIP. 2nd ed. McGraw-Hill, 1977. $13.95.
A clear overall presentation of the fundamentals of librarianship.

Hannaford, Claudia. THE CHURCH AND SYNAGOGUE LIBRARY ASSOCIATION: FIFTEEN YEARS OF QUALITY SERVICE IN RELIGIOUS LIBRARIES. In *Special Libraries,* Vol. 74, no. 3; July, 1983. Special Libraries Association, 235 Park Avenue South, New York, NY 10003. Single copy, $9. Reprint available from CSLA. 40¢ plus stamped, self–addressed envelope.
A description and history of the first 15 years of CSLA.

Harvey, John F., ed. CHURCH AND SYNAGOGUE LIBRARIES. Scarecrow, 1980. $16.50.
A collection of essays on the history and development of congregational librarianship in general and within various faith groups, written by contributors active in the field.

Hicks, Warren B. and Alma M. Tillin. DEVELOPING MULTI–MEDIA LIBRARIES. Bowker, 1970. $8.95.
Discusses the concept of multi–media libraries and gives detailed examples, with illustrations for procedures involving all types of materials.

Hill, Glynn T. HOW TO DEVELOP A MEDIA EDUCATION PROGRAM. Convention, 1981. $1.25.
Guidelines for establishing plans and procedures for teaching church members and leaders the value of using library materials and how to use them correctly.

Mee, Keith. THE LEARNING TEAM: THE LEARNER, THE LEADER, AND THE LIBRARY. Convention, 1976. $4.55.
Shows how media may be related to each facet of the learning process.

SETTING UP A LIBRARY: HOW TO BEGIN OR BEGIN AGAIN. A CSLA slide set. 1983. $75. Rental, $10. 56 color slides; reading script.
Slides and script prepared by Ruth S. Smith, based on CSLA Guide 1 of the same title.

Smith, Ruth S. RUNNING A LIBRARY: MANAGING THE CONGREGATION'S LIBRARY WITH CARE, CONFIDENCE, AND COMMON SENSE. Winston–Seabury, in cooperation with CSLA, 1982. $7.95. (Available from CSLA)
How to effectively create and manage a church or synagogue library.

Smith, Ruth S. WORKSHOP PLANNING. CSLA Guide 3. 2nd ed. Church and Synagogue Library Association, 1979. $6.
Step by step guidance in planning and producing a library workshop for volunteers.

STANDARDS FOR CHURCH AND SYNAGOGUE LIBRARIES: GUIDELINES FOR MEASURING EFFECTIVENESS AND PROGRESS. CSLA Guide 6. Church and Synagogue Library Association, 1977. $3.75.
Suggestions for the wise development of a congregational library and a checklist for long range planning.

TAKE WINGS. Sound filmstrip. Lutheran Church Library Association, 1979. 80 frames. 15 minute cassette. Printed script, by Rolf Aaseng. Usage guide.
May be borrowed free of charge from LCLA. Purpose is to inspire churches to start libraries or improve existing ones.

Tillin, Alma. SCHOOL LIBRARY MEDIA CENTER PROCEDURES. Demco. $2.50.
Clearly written procedures for handling books and audiovisual materials in a small library.

White, Joyce L. CHURCH AND SYNAGOGUE LIBRARIES: RESOURCES FOR THE PUBLIC LIBRARY. In *Library Journal,* Vol. 109, no. 17, October 15, 1984. Bowker. Single Copy, $3.50.
A discussion of the ways that church and synagogue libraries can supplement the services of public libraries in their communities.

# 2.  CHURCH AND SYNAGOGUE LIBRARY MANUALS

Anderson, Jacqulyn. HOW TO ADMINISTER AND PROMOTE A CHURCH MEDIA CENTER. Broadman, 1978. $5.95.
A discussion of the operation and administration of a church media center with emphasis on staff duties, rules, hours, circulation procedures, selection of materials, and the promotion of media and media services.

Beck, Linda. A HANDBOOK FOR CHURCH LIBRARIANS, edited by Miriam Johnson. Parish Life Press, 1982.
Excellent overall presentation of how to start and develop a church library, supplemented with lists of appropriate subject headings and Dewey classification numbers. Good index and bibliography.

Berman, Margot S. HOW TO ORGANIZE A JEWISH LIBRARY: A SOURCE BOOK AND GUIDE FOR SYNAGOGUE, SCHOOL AND CENTER LIBRARIES. JWB Jewish Book Council, 1982. $7.
Includes appendices of definitions, sample materials and sources.

Brown, Charles C. THE SMALL CHURCH LIBRARY: A GUIDE FOR ORGANIZING AND MANAGING IT. Forward Movement Publications, 1981. 95¢ plus 50¢ postage and handling. Includes a simplified cataloging system intended for libraries that are not expected to grow beyond 1,000 volumes.

Corrigan, John T., CFX. GUIDE FOR THE ORGANIZATION AND OPERATION OF A RELIGIOUS RESOURCE CENTER. Catholic Library Association, 1977. $2.50.
Guidelines for the development of a Catholic parish resource center.

Dotts, Maryann J. THE CHURCH RESOURCE LIBRARY: HOW TO START IT AND MAKE IT GROW. Abingdon, 1975. $2.95.
Excellent handbook on the establishment and development of the church library as a resource center. Simplified Dewey schedule and subject headings.

John, Erwin E. THE KEY TO A SUCCESSFUL CHURCH LIBRARY. Rev. ed. Augsburg, 1967. $3.95.
Manual on procedures in starting and operating a church library. Includes author's own classification scheme.

McMichael, Betty, THE CHURCH LIBRARIAN'S HANDBOOK. Baker, 1984. $9.95.
A complete guide for the library and resource center in Christian education, including a chapter on the use of computers in the church library.

Scheer, Gladys E. THE CHURCH LIBRARY: TIPS AND TOOLS. Bethany Press, 1973. $2.50.
Specific "how-to" suggestions for starting and operating a church library. Appendices include a listing of library supplies and equipment companies and a list of denominational services to libraries.

Smith, Ruth S. SETTING UP A LIBRARY: HOW TO BEGIN OR BEGIN AGAIN. CSLA Guide 1. Church and Synagogue Library Association, 1979. $2.50.
An outline of specific steps that will insure a sound and efficient congregational library. Beyond suggestions for defining the purpose and establishing objectives, gaining support and evaluating the program, a bibliography lists additional sources of aid.

Taylor, Lillian McCulloch. A MANUAL FOR CHURCH LIBRARIES. Board of Christian Education, Cumberland Presbyterian Church, 1978 Union Avenue, Memphis, TN 38104. 1983. $2.95.
Basic information on starting a library and brief lists of subject headings and classification numbers.

Walls, Francine E. THE CHURCH LIBRARY WORKBOOK. Light and Life Press, 1980. $8.95.
Step by step guidance plus forms to work out plans for your own library.

# 3. FURNISHING AND EQUIPPING THE LIBRARY

Hill, Glynn T. HOW TO PLAN MEDIA LIBRARY SPACE AND FURNISHINGS. Convention, 1984. $3.50.
Practical guidelines for determining adequate space and furnishings for a church media library. Suggested floor plans are included of minimum medium and large areas of space. Appendix includes drawings with specific dimensions for all types of library furnishings.

For suppliers of library supplies, equipment and furniture, see the following:

THE BAKER AND TAYLOR COMPANIES, 1515 Broadway, New York, NY 10036.
Book wholesalers. Books may be pre-processed.

BRODART INDUSTRIES, INC. Eastern Division, P.O. Box 3037, 1609 Memorial Avenue, Williamsport, PA 17705; Western Division, 1236 Hatcher Street, City of Industry, CA 91748.
Library supplies and furniture, audiovisuals and books, including pre-processed books.

COKESBURY, 201 Eighth Avenue South, Nashville, TN 37202. Many local outlets.
Among many church supplies, books and church library furnishings and equipment. Also, computer books and software.

DEMCO, Box 7488, Madison, WI 53707.
Supplies, furniture, art prints, paperbacks, computer supplies.

GAYLORD BROTHERS, INC. Eastern Division, Box 4901, Syracuse, NY 24302; Western Division, Box 8489, Stockton, CA 95208.
Library supplies and equipment.

THE HIGHSMITH COMPANY, INC. P.O. Box 800A, Highway 106 East, Fort Atkinson, WI 53538.
Furniture and supplies for libraries and offices; also includes computer supplies.

THE SUNDAY SCHOOL BOARD OF THE SOUTHERN BAPTIST CONVENTION, Book Store Division, 127 Ninth Avenue North, Nashville, TN 37234.
Extensive line of church library supplies and equipment.

UNIVERSITY PRODUCTS, INC. P.O. Box 101, South Canal Street, Holyoke, MA 02041.
Library supplies and equipment. Reprint of layout guide for library planning available from CSLA. Send 20¢ plus stamped, self-addressed business envelope.

# 4. SELECTION AND ACQUISITION OF MATERIALS

Adams, Charles, J. READER'S GUIDE TO THE GREAT RELIGIONS. 2nd ed. Free Press, 1977. $24.95.
Annotated subject guide to books on all major religions.

Bonk, Wallace and Rose Magrill. BUILDING LIBRARY COLLECTIONS. 5th ed. Scarecrow, 1979. $13.50.
A standard work in the field of library book selection.

BOOKS IN PRINT. Bowker. Published annually in November.
The available books, new and old, indexed alphabetically in several volumes with authors and titles in separate alphabets. Full ordering information is given. The final title volume includes an alphabetical listing of publishers.

SUBJECT GUIDE TO BOOKS IN PRINT. Bowker. Published annually in November.
A subject index to the previous listing. Both are available at public libraries.

Carsch, Judith S. and Miriam D. Miller. CREATING A COLLECTION: A RESOURCE BOOKLIST FOR A BEGINNING JUDAIC LIBRARY. Association of Jewish Libraries, 1983. $4.
Titles arranged by author under subject categories.

CHILDREN'S BOOKS FOR BIBLE READING AND STUDY, compiled by Bernard E. Deitrick for National Bible Week. Laymen's National Bible Committee, Inc., 815 Second Avenue, Suite 512, New York, NY 10017. 1982. Free. Up to 20 copies available from CSLA.
Graded, annotated subject listing of more than 60 books. Their interest for the three major U.S. faiths: Catholic, Jewish, Protestant, is indicated.

Christian Board of Publication. REVIEW-BY-MAIL PLAN. Box 179, St. Louis, MO 63133.
Registered church libraries receive a quarterly consignment of 5 - 6 books with description and cataloging information. Receive 20% discount on those retained.

COKESBURY CHURCH LIBRARY GUILD, 201 Eighth Avenue South, Nashville, RN 37202.
Enrolled members automatically receive approximately 5 titles per year. Benefits also include a basic book list, 5 issues of *Church Library News* and discounts on purchases.

Deitrick, Bernard E. A BASIC BOOK LIST FOR CHURCH LIBRARIES. A CSLA Bibliography. 2nd rev. ed. Church and Synagogue Library Association, 1983. $3.
An annotated subject list of some 200 books in 22 categories. Includes reference works and children's books. Those especially recommended for a core collection are indicated.

Deitrick, Bernard E. KNOW YOUR NEIGHBOR'S FAITH: AN ANNOTATED INTERFAITH BIBLIOGRAPHY. Church and Synagogue Library Association, 1983. $3.
A listing of books recommended by individuals from various faith groups in North America to help others understand their faith.

HELPFUL BOOKS FOR BIBLE READING AND STUDY, compiled by Bernard E. Deitrick for National Bible Week. Laymen's National Bible Committee, Inc., 815 Second Avenue, Suite 512, New York, NY 10017. 1984. Free. Up to 20 copies available from CSLA.
Annotated subject listing of more than 60 books. Their interest for the three major U.S. faiths: Catholic, Jewish, Protestant, is indicated.

JEWISH BOOK ANNUAL. JWB Jewish Book Council. $18.
Comprehensive bibliographies and useful essays. (Send for complete list of inexpensive subject bibliographies and other aids available from JWB Jewish Book Council.)

LARGE TYPE BOOKS IN PRINT. 5th ed. Bowker, 1982. $35.
A subject listing of over 3,500 books reproduced in large type for easier reading by individuals with visual impairments. A section on religion is included. Author and title indexes. Available in public libraries.

Provident Library Associates Network. PLAN. Provident Bookstores (Mennonite Publishing House). Free enrollment.
Members receive quarterly newsletter, *Network,* bimonthly book review magazine, *Provident Book Finder,* and discounts at Provident Bookstores.

RELIGIOUS BOOKS AND SERIALS IN PRINT. 3rd ed. Bowker, 1983. $69.50.
A subject listing of more than 50,000 titles in all religions and related fields. Includes a separate Bible section, author and title indexes, separate indexes for children's and religious fiction, and a directory of all publishers represented with current addresses. Published biennially in the fall. Available in public libraries.

Swarthout, Arthur W. SELECTING LIBRARY MATERIALS. CSLA Guide 4. Rev. ed. Church and Synagogue Library Association, 1978. $2.50.
An outline guide to the selection and acquisition of congregational library materials with specific suggestions of review sources and publishers. A checklist, sample selection policy statement and bibliography are appended.

Posner, Marcia. SELECTED JEWISH CHILDREN'S BOOKS. Rev. ed. JWB Jewish Book Council, 1984. $5.
An annotated list of 250 books, fiction and non-fiction, for pre-school to young adult.

Tuchman, Helene L. LARGE PRINT BOOKS OF JEWISH INTEREST. Rev. ed. JWB Jewish Book Council, 1983. $4.
A list of fiction and non-fiction sources for large print material.

Weber, J. Sherwood, ed. GOOD READING: A GUIDE FOR SERIOUS READERS. 21st ed. Bowker, 1978. $1.50. Paper, New American Library, 1980. $3.50.
Lists by subject, annotates, evaluates, and provides full bibliographic data on 2,500 carefully selected books.

Wulfekoetter, Gertrude. ACQUISITION WORK: PROCESSES INVOLVED IN BUILDING LIBRARY COLLECTIONS. U. of Washington Press, Seattle, WA 98105. 1962. $16.50.
A basic work on the subject which has been re-issued repeatedly.

For Children:

CHILDREN'S BOOKS IN PRINT. Bowker. Published annually.
Provides author-title-illustrator indexes to some 40,000 children's books, from pre-school through grade 12. Directory of publishers. Available in public libraries.

SUBJECT GUIDE TO CHILDREN'S BOOKS IN PRINT. Bowker. Published annually.
A subject arranged companion to the previous listing.

Gillespie, John T. and C. Gilbert, eds. BEST BOOKS FOR CHILDREN. 2nd ed. Bowker, 1981. $29.95.
A selection of titles that support current curriculum and reading interests. Helpful in building a core library of children's books or choosing books of individual interest.

Hearne, Betsy. CHOOSING BOOKS FOR CHILDREN: A COMMON SENSE GUIDE. Delacorte 1981. $8.95.

Karp, Hazel and Ellen Rosenthal. JEWISH CHIL-
DREN'S BOOKS: A SELECTED BIBLIOGRAPHY
OF 100 BOOKS FOR A BEGINNING LIBRARY.
Association of Jewish Libraries, 1983. $3.50.
Frequently updated, annotated bibliography.

Larrick, Nancy. A PARENT'S GUIDE TO CHIL-
DREN'S READING. 5th ed. Westminster, 1982.
$12.95.
A standard list prepared and frequently updated
by the winner of the 1984 CSLA Helen Keating
Ott Award for outstanding contribution to chil-
dren's literature.

Ott, Helen Keating Ott. HELPING CHILDREN
THROUGH BOOKS: A SELECTED BOOKLIST.
A CSLA Bibliography. Rev. ed. Church and Synagogue Library Association, 1979. $3.75.
A grade annotated subject list of books for children, related to their personal and social development.

Pearl, Patricia. RELIGIOUS BOOKS FOR CHIL-
DREN. A CSLA Bibliography. Church and Synagogue Library Association, 1983. $5.
A graded, critically annotated subject listing of
children's books dealing with religion or having a
strong overt religious theme.

# 5. PERIODICALS
# FOR THE CONGREGATIONAL LIBRARIAN

AJL NEWSLETTER. Quarterly. Association of Jewish Libraries. Subscription free with membership
in Association. $18.
Articles, book and media reviews.

AMERICAN BOOK PUBLISHING RECORD. Monthly. Bowker. Subscription $55 per year.
Cumulates by subject (Dewey Decimal arrange-
ment) all books listed during the current month in
*Weekly Record.* Entries give published price,
Dewey Decimal number, Library of Congress subject headings, catalog card and classification numbers, publisher, whether illustrated, etc. Available
in public libraries.

BOOK NEWSLETTER. Bimonthly. Augsburg Publishing House. Free.
Reviews of books from various publishers.

THE CALENDAR. Quarterly. Children's Book Council. $15 one time fee.
Includes new book titles relating to important
dates within the quarter, free and inexpensive
materials for display or promotion and other
information related to children's literature.

CATHOLIC LIBRARY WORLD. Monthly (10 issues
per year). Catholic Library Association. Subscription $30 per year or free with memberships.
Articles, news items and book reviews relating to
all Catholic libraries. Newsletter of Parish and
Community Libraries section free with membership if you elect to receive it as your one special
interest section.

CATHOLIC PERIODICAL AND LITERATURE IN-
DEX. Bimonthly. Catholic Library Association.
$45 basic rate.
An author and subject index to 142 Catholic periodicals and national Catholic newspapers and
books by Catholics and other authors whose work
is of Catholic interest.

CATHOLIC PERIODICAL AND LITERATURE IN-
DEX — ABRIDGED EDITION. Bimonthly. Catholic Library Association. $30 basic rate.
Indexes 35 periodicals, book titles and annotations
and is intended for smaller, parish libraries and
religious education centers.

CHRISTIAN BOOKSELLER. Monthly. Christian Life
Missions, 396 E. St. Charles Road, Wheaton, IL
60187. $18 per year.
Book and media reviews. Column for church
librarians.

CHRISTIAN PERIODICAL INDEX. Quarterly with
annual cumulations. Christian Librarians' Fellow-
ship. $32 per year.
An author–subject index to over 50 Christian
periodicals (including *Church and Synagogue
Libraries).* For information, write: Ruth G. Butler,
Houghton College, Buffalo Campus, 910 Union
Road, West Seneca, NY  14224.

CHURCH AND SYNAGOGUE LIBRARIES. Bi-monthly. Church and Synagogue Library Association. Subscription $15. per year or free with memberships. Church or synagogue members receive 3 copies; institutional or affiliated members, 5 copies.
articles, news, book and media reviews for church and synagogue librarians.

CHURCH LIBRARY NEWS. 5 times per year. Cokesbury Church Library Association. $7.50 annually or free with membership.
News and reviews for church librarians.

Corrigan, John T., C.F.X., editor. PERIODICALS FOR RELIGIOUS EDUCATION CENTERS AND PARISH LIBRARIES: A GUIDE TO MAGAZINES, NEWSPAPERS AND NEWSLETTERS. Catholic Library Association, 1976. $3.
Identifies and evaluates 106 periodicals recommended for religious education centers, parish and other libraries with religion collections. Also evaluates media selection sources. Ordering information included.

THE HORN BOOK MAGAZINE. Bimonthly. The Horn Book, Inc. $25. per year.
Articles and reviews of children's books.

JED SHARE. Quarterly. United Church Press for Joint Education Development, 132 W. 31st Street, New York, NY 10001. $7. per year.
An exchange of Christian education ideas, programs resources and concern shared by the co-sponsoring denominations. Book reviews.

JUDAICA BOOK NEWS. Semi-annual. Write to Book News, Inc., 303 West 10th Street, New York, NY 10014 or obtain at local Jewish bookstores. $7. per year.
Listings of new Jewish books.

JUDAICA LIBRARIANSHIP . Association of Jewish Libraries, 17201 North East 11th Court, North Miami Beach, FL 33162.

LIBRARIAN'S WORLD. Quarterly. Evangelical Church Library Association. Free with membership; dues, $7. per year.
Articles, news and book reviews for church librarians.

LIBRARY JOURNAL. Semi-monthly (20 issues per year). Bowker. $59 per year.
Extensive book review section, arranged by subject. Special religious book issues. Available in public libraries.

LUTHERAN LIBRARIES. Quarterly. Lutheran Church Library Association. Free with membership; personal dues $15 per year.
Articles and news of interest to church librarians. Regular "Books in Review" section includes Dewey Decimal classification number and subject headings for each book. Non-book material also reviewed.

MEDIA: LIBRARY SERVICES JOURNAL. Quarterly. Sunday School Board, Southern Baptist Convention. $6.75 per year.
Contains articles and features including promotional ideas and technical guidance for church media library workers. Recommendations of new materials include annotations and Dewey Decimal classification numbers and suggested subject headings. Annual index.

NETWORK. Quarterly. Provident Library Associates Network (PLAN). Free with enrollment in PLAN. Newsletter designed to provide practical help for cataloging, displaying, and promoting books in the library. Idea exchange.

PROVIDENT BOOK FINDER. Bimonthly. Provident Bookstores, 616 Walnut Street, Scottdale, PA 15683. Free to members of PLAN and regular customers of Provident Bookstores. Others invited to contribute $5 for 2 years.
Reviews of books of various publishers of interest to religious libraries.

PUBLISHERS WEEKLY. Bowker. $78. per year.
Information about forth coming publications. See especially semi-annual religious issues in public library.

REVIEW OF BOOKS AND RELIGION. Kendig Brubaker Cully, editor, Divinity School, Duke University, Durham, NC 27706. 10 times per year. $16.
General articles on trends in religious publishing and reviews of books from all publishers.

# 6. NON-BOOK MATERIALS

Anderson, Jacqulyn. DEVELOPING A CHURCH MUSIC LIBRARY. Convention, 1983. $4.80. Guidance for processing and cataloging choir music including octavos, cantatas, collections, and other music. The system provides for subject cataloging and enables all music to be accessible by title, composer, subject, age grouping, and voicing.

Anderson, Jacqulyn. HOW TO PROCESS MEDIA. Broadman. $5.75.
Basic information on processing and cataloging all media center materials for circulation.

AUDIOVISUAL MARKET PLACE 1983: MULTI-MEDIA GUIDE. Bowker. $39.95.
Identifies some 5,000 firms and individuals now active in 25 areas of AV goods and services including hardware and software producers and distributors. Available in public libraries.

Hack, John. HOW TO MAKE AUDIOVISUALS. Broadman, 1973. $5.75.
A practical guide for media center workers, teachers, and others in the making and presenting of audiovisuals. Includes chapters on slides, tapes, overhead transparencies, and other types of audiovisuals.

Hack, John. HOW TO OPERATE A CASSETTE TAPE MINISTRY. Broadman, 1979. $4.25. Gives instruction on setting up and operating a program of providing cassette tapes of services and special messages and music for the homebound and others. Includes information about tape masters, duplication, and other pertinent matters.

Heubner, Mary A. NON-BOOK MATERIALS IN THE LIBRARY. Library Services Board, Lutheran Church Library Association. $3.
How to process, catalog, store and circulate non-book materials of all kinds.

Jensen, Mary and Andrew Jensen. AUDIOVISUAL IDEA BOOK FOR CHURCHES. Augsburg, 1974. $5.50.
The effective use of audiovisual aids in church programs.

Johnson, Jean Thornton and others. A-V CATALOGING AND PROCESSING SIMPLIFIED. Audiovisual Cataloguers, Inc., P. O. Box 26002, Raleigh, NC 27611.

Korty, Margaret Barton. AUDIOVISUAL MATERIALS IN THE CHURCH LIBRARY: HOW TO SELECT, CATALOG, PROCESS, STORE, CIRCULATE AND PROMOTE. Church Library Council, 1977. $4.95. On approval, 50¢ extra. Chapters on administration, general treatment, films, filmstrips, slides, overhead transparencies, opaque projection, stereo reels and viewstrips, phonograph records, tape recordings, pictures, maps, and miscellaneous visual aids.

MEDIUM. Quarterly. Jewish Media Service, 15 East 26th Street, New York, NY 10010. $15. per year. Newsletter reviewing films and other audio-visual forms on subjects of interest to religious educators, program planners and librarians.

Mee, Keith. HOW TO USE AUDIOVISUALS. Convention, 1983. $4.55.
Guidance for teachers and learners.

PREVIEWS: NEWS AND REVIEWS OF NON-PRINT MEDIA. Bowker. Monthly. $7.50.

Tillin, Alma and William J. Quinly. STANDARDS FOR CATALOGING NON-PRINT MATERIALS. 4th ed. $8.95. Association for Educational Communications and Technology, 1126 Sixteenth St. NW, Washington, DC 20036.

Weihs, Jean. ACCESSIBLE STORAGE OF NON-BOOK MATERIALS. Oryx, 1984. $19.50.
Suggestions for making nonbook materials accessible for browsing, while ensuring safe, orderly storage. Covers full range of AV's.

# 7. TECHNICAL AIDS

Anderson, Jacqulyn. HOW TO CLASSIFY, CATA-LOG, AND MAINTAIN MEDIA. Broadman, 1978. $5.95.
A detailed, in-depth study of classification, cataloging, subject cataloging, and book and audiovisual repair and maintenance. The use of the Dewey Decimal classification system and *Sears List of Subject Headings* are covered.

Anderson, Jacqulyn. DEWEY DECIMAL AND SEARS UPDATE. Broadman, 1981. $2.75.
An updated supplement to *How to Classify, Catalog, and Maintain Media.*

Anderson, Jacqulyn. HOW TO PROCESS MEDIA. Broadman, 1978. $5.95.
A Step-by-step illustrated guide giving the procedures for processing books, audiovisuals, vertical file items, and miscellaneous materials. Covers the basic aspects of cataloging materials and setting up a card catalog.

Anderson, Jacqulyn. MEDIA CENTER TECHNI-QUES (cassette tapes). Broadman, 1978. Set, $24.95; each tape, $6.95.
(1) Classifying Books for the Church Media Center.
(2) Cataloging Materials for the Church Media Center.
(3) Subject Cataloging in the Church Media Center.
(4) Making and Using Cross Reference Cards.
Provides further guidance and training in the technical areas of media center work, using the book *How to Classify, Catalog, and Maintain Media* as the basis of the study. Worksheets are included.

BOOK CRAFT. Gaylord. Free on request.
Illustrated manual describing various methods of book repairing and periodical binding.

BOOK PRESERVATION AND REPAIR GUIDE. Demco. $2.50.
Step-by-step instructions necessary to complete your own book repairs as well as prepare new books for longer circulation.

CATALOGUE CARD ASSEMBLER, a computer program prepared by Sharyn Van Epps and Jon Mauch, Madeira Schools, Cincinnati, Ohio 45243. 1983. $78. May be used on Apple II or Apple IIe / Dos 3.3
Will print a complete set of library cards, book card and labels for book spine and pocket. Will print out bibliography. 92 books may be entered on a disk, at the rate of about 15 an hour.

CHURCH MEDIA LIBRARY RECORD AND PLAN BOOK. Convention, 1983. $1.60.
For planning promotional and educational activities and keeping records of media library circulation, finances, staff information, and other data. Guidelines for planning and utilizing records are also included.

CLASSIFICATION AND CATALOGING GUIDE. 5th ed. Broadman, 1982. $11.95.
Provides technical help for media library workers by listing classification numbers and subject headings for media library materials, both printed and audiovisual.

SUPPLEMENT: CLASSIFICATION AND CATA-LOGING GUIDE. 5th ed. Broadman, 1984. $4.95.

Curley, Arthur and Jana Varlejs. AKERS' SIMPLE LIBRARY CATALOGING. 7th ed. Scarecrow, 1984. $16.50.
Standard guide for the small library without a professional cataloguer. New edition still firmly rooted in practicality enhanced by recognition that small libraries, too, are part of the modern age.

Dewey, Melvil. DEWEY DECIMAL CLASSIFICA-TION AND RELATIVE INDEX. 11th abridged edition. Wilson, 1979. $27.
An abridgment of the full schedules of the Dewey Decimal Classification, intended for small libraries of all sorts. Contains introductory section on book classification.

Dewey, Melvil. 200 (RELIGION) CLASS. DEWEY DECIMAL CLASSIFICATION. Broadman, 1980. $4.50.
The unabridged religion section reprinted from the 19th unabridged edition of the Dewey Decimal Classification. Recommended for use in conjunction with the abridged edition of DDC. Indexed.

Gorman, Michael and Paul Winkler. ANGLO AMERI-CAN CATALOGING RULES II. 2nd ed. American Library Association, 1978. $20. Paper, $15.
Although most congregational libraries will not feel the need of the detail suggested, AACR II is de-

signed for computer use, so some may wish to follow codes for future automating or interlibrary cooperation.

Kersten, Dorothy B. CLASSIFYING CHURCH OR SYNAGOGUE LIBRARY MATERIALS. CSLA Guide 7. Church and Synagogue Library Association, rev. 1982. $2.50.
An explanation of classification procedures, followed by a listing of the Dewey Decimal classification numbers most likely to be used in a congregational library.

Kersten, Dorothy B. SUBJECT HEADINGS FOR CHURCH OR SYNAGOGUE LIBRARIES. CSLA Guide 8. Church and Synagogue Library Association, rev. 1984. $3.50.
An introduction to subject cataloging, with a list of subject headings that are most likely to be used in a congregational library. Suggested Dewey Decimal classification numbers are listed with each subject heading.

LIBRARIAN'S HELPER. A computer program developed by Bob Pritchett & Co., 23 Pawtucket Drive, Cherry Hill, NJ 08003, especially for church libraries. 1983. $50. Can be used on 36 different kinds of computers.
Generates complete sets of catalog cards and labels for book spine, book pocket and card.

Miller, Rosalind and Jane Terwilleger. COMMON-SENSE CATALOGING. 3rd ed. Wilson, 1983. $22.
Third revision of the original work by Esther Piercey. Practical illustrated handbook for the beginning cataloger, trained or untrained. Chapters on general procedures and each step of the cataloging process.

MODERN SIMPLIFIED BOOK REPAIR. Brodart. Free upon request.
Directions for repairing worn materials.

Pilley, Catherine M. and Matthew R. Wilt, eds. CATHOLIC SUBJECT HEADINGS. Catholic Library Association, 1981. $25.
A current list of Catholic subject headings reflecting the terminology changes since Vatican II.

Ruoss, G. Martin. A POLICY AND PROCEDURE MANUAL FOR CHURCH AND SYNAGOGUE LIBRARIES: A DO-IT-YOURSELF GUIDE. CSLA Guide 9. Church and Synagogue Library Association, 1979. $3.75.
How to set up a manual of policies and procedures for your library.

Seely, Pauline A., ed. ALA RULES FOR FILING CATALOG CARDS. 2nd edition abridged. American Library Association, 1968. $5.
A good, practical presentation of the subject.

Segal, Joseph P. EVALUATING AND WEEDING COLLECTIONS IN SMALL AND MEDIUM-SIZED PUBLIC LIBRARIES: THE CREW METHOD. American Library Association, 1980. $3.
The single, most helpful manual on why and how to maintain your library through taking inventory and weeding. Readily adaptable to use in congregational libraries.

Skanse, Ruth T. THE CHURCH LIBRARY SERIES. Evangelical Church Library Association. $5.
Compilation of 24 articles on library practice that originally appeared in the official bulletin of ECLA, *Librarians World.*

Smith, Ruth S. CATALOGING BOOKS STEP BY STEP. CSLA Guide 5. Church and Synagogue Library Association, 1977. $2.50.
Outline guidance in preparing books for circulation in a library. Sample catalog cards and a glossary of cataloging terms are appended.

Stuhlman, Daniel D. LIBRARY OF CONGRESS SUBJECT HEADINGS FOR JUDAICA. BYLS Press, (6247 N. Francisco Avenue, Chicago, IL 60659), 1982. $6. 1983 Update, $1.50.

Weine, Mae and Mildred Kurland, Eds. WEINE CLASSIFICATION SYSTEM. Association of Jewish Libraries. $12.50 for 3 volume set.
CLASSIFICATION SCHEME FOR JUDAICA LIBRARIES. 7th ed. 1982. $6.
SUBJECT HEADINGS FOR A JUDAICA LIBRARY. 4th ed. 1982. $6.
RELATIVE INDEX TO THE WEINE CLASSIFICATION SCHEME FOR JUDAICA LIBRARIES. 1982.

Westby, Barbara M. SEARS LIST OF SUBJECT HEADINGS. 12th ed. Wilson, 1982. $25.
A comprehensive list of general subject headings appropriate for small and medium-sized libraries. Contains introductory section of practical suggestions for the beginner in subject heading work.

# 8. PROMOTION AND PUBLICITY

Coplan, Kate et al. POSTER IDEAS AND BULLE-TIN BOARD TECHNIQUES. Rev. ed. Oceana, 1981. $25.

Coplan, Kate and Constance Rosenthal. GUIDE TO BETTER BULLETIN BOARDS. Oceana, 1970. $20.
Ideas for bulletin boards and displays. Suggestions for using discarded materials.

Ezell, Mancel and Charles Businaro. PROMOTION HANDBOOK FOR CHURCH MEDIA LIBRAR-IES. Convention, 1984. $8.95.
Guide for promoting a church media library with practical suggestions for preparing posters, bulletin boards, displays and other means of informing church leaders and members about the media library. Planning calendar included.

THE FAMILY USES THE LIBRARY. Church and Synagogue Library Association. 5¢ per copy; $3.75/100; $15/500.
A 4-page leaflet suitable for bulletin enclosure or other quantity distribution, inviting use and support of the congregational library.

Garvey, Mona. LIBRARY DISPLAYS. Wilson, 1969. $12.
Specific helps in creating one's own designs and in easy methods of lettering and cartooning.

Hannaford, Claudia and Ruth S. Smith. PROMO-TION PLANNING ALL YEAR 'ROUND. CSLA Guide 2. Rev. 2nd ed. Church and Synagogue Library Association, 1978. $4.50.
A guide for relating congregational library publi-city to the events of the year. The programs and activities suggested have been used successfully.

HOW TO EXPAND MEDIA LIBRARY SERVICES. Convention, 1984. $2.75.
How to identify opportunities for your media library to enhance the work of your church.

MEDIA LIBRARY POSTER SET. Broadman, 1984.
A set of 6 two-color posters, 17 x 22, to use in promoting a church media library, its materials and services.

Paris, Janelle. PLANNING BULLETIN BOARDS FOR CHURCH AND SYNAGOGUE LIBRARIES. CSLA Guide 11. Church and Synagogue Library A to Z on how to prepare bulletin boards and use them effectively for library promotion.

PROMOTION PLANNING ALL YEAR 'ROUND. A CSLA slide set. 100 35mm slides; cassette; read-ing script. Church and Synagogue Library Associa-tion, 1983. $100; rental, $15.
Slides, cassette and script prepared by Claudia Hannaford, based on CSLA Guide 2 of the same title.

THE TEACHER AND THE LIBRARY — PART-NERS IN RELIGIOUS EDUCATION. Church and Synagogue Library Association. 10¢ per copy; $2/25; $3.75/50; $7/100.
A four-page illustrated tract designed for distribu-tion to religious education teachers to encourage them to incorporate the services of a media center in their teaching.

For additional promotional ideas, see the following sources:

AMERICAN BIBLE SOCIETY, 1865 Broadway, New York, NY 10023.
Display materials and poster sets relating to the Bible. Some may be borrowed free of charge.

CHILDREN'S BOOK COUNCIL, INC., 67 Irving Place, New York, NY 10003.
Sponsors of CHILDREN'S BOOK WEEK annually in the fall. Write for promotion and publicity aids by August.

JWB JEWISH BOOK COUNCIL, 15 East 26th Street, New York, NY 10001.
Sponsors JEWISH BOOK MONTH annually in the fall. Publications and materials available.

LAYMEN'S NATIONAL BIBLE COMMITTEE, INC., 815 Second Avenue, Suite 512, New York, NY 10017.
Sponsors of NATIONAL BIBLE WEEK annually in the fall. Promotional materials available free of charge, including two bibliographies of Bible study aids, one for adults and one for children, prepared by the Church and Synagogue Library Association.

NATIONAL LIBRARY WEEK PARTNERS. An association of more than 40 national groups, including CSLA, interested in promoting reading. Sponsors NATIONAL LIBRARY WEEK annually in the spring. Write for promotion and publicity aids by February to 1564 Broadway, New York, NY 10036.

UPSTART LIBRARY PROMOTIONALS, Box 889, Hagerstown, MD 21741.
Promotional aids including materials for NATIONAL LIBRARY WEEK.

# 9. ARCHIVES

Corrigan, John T., CFX, editor. ARCHIVES: THE LIGHT OF FAITH. CLA Studies in Librarianship No. 5. Catholic Library Association, 1981. $4.
A discussion of the place of archieves in the framework of church history.

Ling, Evelyn R. ARCHIVES IN THE CHURCH OR SYNAGOGUE LIBRARY. CSLA Guide 11. Church and Synagogue Library Association, 1981. $4.50.
How to establish and make use of archives in your congregation.

Suelflow, August R. RELIGIOUS ARCHIVES: AN INTRODUCTION. SAA Basic Archival Manual Series. 1980. Society of American Archivists, 330 S. Wells St., Suite 810, Chicago, IL 60606.

Thompson, Enid T. LOCAL HISTORY: A MANUAL FOR LIBRARIANS. 1978. $7.95. American Association for State and Local History, 1400 Eighth Avenue South, Nashville, TN 37203.
Helpful guidance for untrained archivists.

For information about archival helps available from various denominations and faith groups, consult the *Yearbook of American and Canadian Churches,* published annually by Abingdon.

# 10. CHURCH AND SYNAGOGUE LIBRARY ASSOCIATIONS

ASSOCIATION OF JEWISH LIBRARIES, 17201 NE 111th Court, North Miami Beach, FL 33162. Order materials from AJL, c/o National Foundation for Jewish Culture, 122 E. 42nd St., Room 1512, New York, NY 10168.
Quarterly: AJL Newsletter

CATHOLIC LIBRARY ASSOCIATION, 461 Lancaster Avenue, Haverford, PA 19041.
10 times per year: Catholic Library World
3 times per year: Parish and Community Library News

CHURCH AND SYNAGOGUE LIBRARIANS' FELLOWSHIP, c/o Miriam Hyde, 3800 Donerin Way, Phoenix, MD 21131.
Quarterly bulletin: Cross and Star.

CHURCH AND SYNAGOGUE LIBRARY ASSOCIATION, P.O. Box 1130, Bryn Mawr, PA 19010.
Bimonthly bulletin: Church and Synagogue Libraries.

CHURCH LIBRARY ASSOCIATION, c/o M. C. Henderson, 10 Allanhurst Drive, Apt. 302, Islington, Ontario M9A 4J5, Canada.

CHURCH LIBRARY COUNCIL, c/o Margaret Korty, 5406 Quintana Street, Riverdale, MD 20840.
Quarterly bulletin: Church Library Council News.

CHURCH LIBRARY DEPARTMENT, SOUTHERN BAPTIST CONVENTION, 127 Ninth Avenue North, Nashville, TN 37234.
Quarterly magazine: Media: Library Services Journal.

COKESBURY CHURCH LIBRARY ASSOCIATION,
201 Eighth Avenue South, Room 248, Nashville,
TN 37202.
Newsletter published five times a year: Church
Library News.

CONGREGATIONAL LIBRARIES ASSOCIATION
OF BRITISH COLUMBIA, c/o Fran Rose, 1860
San Juan Avenue, Victoria, B.C. V8N 2J2, Canada.
Quarterly bulletin: The Rare Bird

EVANGELICAL CHURCH LIBRARY ASSOCIA-
TION, P.O. Box 353, Glen Ellyn, IL 60137.
Quarterly bulletin: Librarians' World.

LUTHERAN CHURCH LIBRARY ASSOCIATION,
122 West Franklin Avenue, Minneapolis, MN
55405.
Quarterly journal: Lutheran Libraries

NORTHERN VIRGINIA CHURCH AND SYNA-
GOGUE LIBRARY COUNCIL, c/o Lynne Thompson, 4219 Burke Station Road, Fairfax, VA 22032.

PACIFIC NORTHWEST ASSOCIATION OF CHURCH LI-
BRARIES. P.O. Box 12379, Main Office Station,
Seattle, WA 98111.
Quarterly bulletin: The Lamplighter.

# AUDIOVISUAL RESOURCE LIST

ALBA HOUSE, Canfield, OH 44406
Films, filmstrips, records, cassettes on Bible study
and contemporary issues.

AMERICAN BIBLE SOCIETY, 1865 Broadway,
New York, NY 10023
Films, filmstrips, cassettes, records, posters, charts
relating to the Bible.

ANTI-DEFAMATION LEAGUE OF B'NAI B'RITH,
823 UN Plaza, New York, NY 10017
Videocassettes, film, filmstrips on human relation-
ships.

ARGUS COMMUNICATIONS, One DLM Park, Box
7000, Allen, TX 75002.

BAUMAN BIBLE TELECASTS, 3436 Lee Highway,
Arlington, VA 22207.
Films and filmstrips, videocassettes on biblical
subjects.

BROADMAN FILMS, 127 Ninth Avenue North,
Nashville, TN 37234.
Bible map transparencies, films, filmstrips.

CATHEDRAL FILMS, P.O. Box 1608, Burbank,
CA 91507.
Films and filmstrips on religious and social issues.

CHRISTIAN CHURCH (DISCIPLES OF CHRIST),
Office of Communication, Box 1986, Indianapolis,
IN 46206.
Silent and sound filmstrips, 16mm films, slides,
videocassettes, audiocassettes.

CHRISTIAN CINEMA, INC. 108 Butler Pike, Ambler,
PA 19002.
Films, filmstrips, transparencies, records.

COKESBURY REGIONAL SERVICE CENTER, 201
Eighth Avenue South, Nashville, TN 37202.
Bible maps, Bible map transparencies, filmstrips,
records, cassettes, pictures.

CONCORDIA PUBLISHING HOUSE, 3558 S. Jefferson Avenue, St. Louis, MO 63118.
Films, filmstrips.

DAVID C. COOK PUBLISHING COMPANY, 850
North Grove Avenue, Elgin, IL 60120.
Cassettes, pictures, maps, records, multi-media
kits of Bible stories.

CREATIVE RESOURCES. Word, Inc., Box 1790,
Waco, TX 76703.
Records, cassette study programs, inspirational
tape series, contemporary issues tapes.

EYE GATE HOUSE, 146-01 Archer Avenue, Jamai-
ca, NY 11435.
High quality sound filmstrips on Bible and religion.

FRIENDSHIP PRESS, Distribution Office, P.O. Box 37844, Cincinnati, OH 45237.
Maps, pictures, books on world issues.

GAYLORD BROTHERS, INC., P.O. Box 4901, Syracuse, NY 13221.
High quality art prints.

GUIDANCE ASSOCIATES, Box 3000 Communications Pk., Mount Kisco, NY 10549.
Filmstrips, multi-media kits, slides on personal development.

THOMAS S. KLISE COMPANY, Box 3418, Peoria, IL 61614.
Sound filmstrips on religion and social problems.

LUTHERAN FILM ASSOCIATES, 360 Park Avenue South, New York, NY 10010.
Films, filmstrips, videocassettes.

MASS MEDIA MINISTRIES, 2116 North Charles Street, Baltimore, MD 21218.
Rental films, filmstrips for purchase.

NATIONAL CATHOLIC REPORTER, Dept. CC, 115 East Armour Boulevard, Kansas City, MO 64141.
Cassette ministry includes reconciliation, music, worship, family life.

PENNSYLVANIA EDUCATIONAL AIDS, 306 East Carson Street, Pittsburgh, PA 15219.
Extensive collection on religious themes.

SACRED FILM LIBRARY, P.O. Box 1269, West Chester, PA 19380.
Rental films.

SOCIETY FOR VISUAL EDUCATION (SVE), 1345 Diversey Parkway, Chicago, IL 60614.
Filmstrips on religions around the world, records, study prints.

TELEKETICS, Franciscan Communication Center, 1229 South Santee Street, Los Angeles, CA 90015.
Films, sound filmstrips and sound slide sets; animated Bible study, social issues.

TWENTY-THIRD PUBLICATIONS, P.O. Box 180, Mystic, CT 06355.
Filmstrips, multi-media kits, records, audio-cassettes.

WINSTON SEABURY PRESS, 430 Oak Grove, Minneapolis, MN 55403.
Sound filmstrips on Christian education.

# DIRECTORY OF PUBLISHERS

Following is a list of suppliers of library materials and major publishers of religious books, including those listed in this bibliography. A complete list of publishers may be found in *Literary Market Place,* published annually by Bowker.

Abbey Press
9 Hill Drive
St. Meinrad, IN 47577

Abingdon Press
201 Eighth Avenue, South
Nashville, TN 37202
(Retail sales through Cokesbury)

Alba House
2187 Victory Boulevard
Staten Island, NY 10314

American Bible Society
1865 Broadway
New York, NY 10023

American Library Association
50 East Huron Street
Chicago, IL 60611

Anti-Defamation League of B'nai B'rith
823 United Nations Plaza
New York, NY 10017

Association of Jewish Libraries
Order materials from:
c/o National Foundation for Jewish Culture
122 East 42nd Street, Room 1512
New York, NY 10168

Augsburg Publishing House
426 South 5th Street
Minneapolis, MN 55440

Ave Maria Press
Notre Dame, IN 46556

Baker Book House
Box 6287
Grand Rapids, MI 49506

Basic Books, Inc.
10 East 53rd Street
New York, NY 10022

Beacon Press
25 Beacon Street
Boston, MA 02108

Bethany House
6820 Auto Club Road
Minneapolis, MN 55438

Bloch Publishing Company
19 West 21st Street
New York, NY 10017

R. R. Bowker Company
205 East 42nd Street
New York, NY 10017

The Brethren Press
1451 Dundee Avenue
Elgin, IL 60120

Broadman Press
127 Ninth Avenue, North
Nashville, TN 37234

CBP Publishers (formerly Bethany Press)
2721 Pine Street, Box 179
St. Louis, MO 63166

Christian Herald Books
40 Overlook Drive
Chappaqua, NY 10514

Cokesbury
201 Eighth Avenue, South
Nashville, TN 37202
    (Retail distributor for several
    denominations)

Concordia Publishing House
3558 South Jefferson Avenue
St. Louis, MO 63118

Convention Press
127 Ninth Avenue, North
Nashville, TN 37234

David C. Cook Publishing Company
850 North Grove Avenue
Elgin, IL 60120

Crossroad Publishing Company
575 Lexington Avenue
New York, NY 10022

Delacorte Press
c/o Dell Publishing Co.
1 Dag Hammarskjol Plaza
245 E. 47th Street
New York, NY 10017

Doubleday & Co.
501 Franklin Avenue
Garden City, NY 11530

Wm. B. Eerdmans Publishing Co.
255 Jefferson Avenue, SE
Grand Rapids, MI 49503

Fortress Press
2900 Queen Lane
Philadelphia, PA 19129

Forward Movement Publications
412 Sycamore Street
Cincinnati, OH 45202

Free Press, Division of Macmillan
866 Third Avenue
New York, NY 10022

Friends United Press
101 Quaker Hill Drive
Richmond, IN 47374

Friendship Press
475 Riverside Drive
New York, NY 10015

Gale Research Company
Penobscot Building
Detroit, MI 48226

Gospel Publishing House
1445 Boonville Avenue
Springfield, MO 65802

Greenwood Press
51 Riverside Avenue
Westport, CT 06880

Harper & Row
1700 Montgomery Street
San Francisco, CA 94111

Herald Press
616 Walnut Avenue
Scottdale, PA 15683

Inter-Varsity Press
Box F
Downers Grove, IL 60515

Jewish Publication Society of
America
1930 Chestnut Street
Philadelphia, PA 19103

John Knox Press
341 Ponce de Leon Avenue NE
Atlanta, GA 30365

John Milton Society for the Blind
475 Riverside Drive
New York, NY 10015

Judson Press
Valley Forge, PA 19481

JWB Jewish Book Council
15 E. 26th Street
New York, NY 10010

KTAV Publishing House
75 Varick Street
New York, NY 10013

Libraries Unlimited
P.O. Box 263
Littleton, CO 80160

Light and Life Press
Winona, IN 46590

Logos International
201 Church Street
Plainfield, NJ 07060

McGraw-Hill
1224 Avenue of the Americas
New York, NY 10020

Mennonite Publishing House
616 Walnut Avenue
Scottdale, PA 15683

Moody Press
2101 West Howard Street
Chicago, IL 60645

Morehouse-Barlow Company
78 Danbury Road
Wilton, CT 06897

Multnomah Press
5600 NE Hassalo Street
Portland, OR 97213

Nazarene Publishing House
Box 527
Kansas City, MO 64141

New American Library
1633 Broadway
New York, NY 10019

Oceana Publications
Dobbs Ferry, NY 10522

Orbis Books
Maryknoll, NY 10545

Oryx Press
2214 N. Central at Encanto, Suite 103
Phoenix, AZ 85004

Our Sunday Visitor Press
200 Noll Plaza
Huntington, IN 46750

Pacific Press Publishing Association
P.O. Box 7000
Mountain View, CA 94039

Parish Life Press
2900 Queen Lane
Philadelphia, PA 19129

Paulist Press
545 Island Road
Ramsey, NJ 07446

Pilgrim Press
132 W. 31st Street
New York, NY 10001

Plough Publishing House
Rifton, NY 12471

Prentice-Hall
Route 9-W
Englewood Cliffs, NJ 07632

Regal Books
2300 Knoll Drive
Ventura, CA 93003

Fleming H. Revell
184 Central Avenue
Old Tappan, NJ 07675

Scarecrow Press
52 Liberty Street, P.O. Box 656
Metuchen, NJ 08844

Schocken Books
200 Madison Avenue
New York, NY 10016

Standard Publishing Company
8121 Hamilton Avenue
Cincinnati, OH 45231

Thomas Nelson Publishers
Nelson Place at Elm Hill Pike
P.O. Box 141000
Nashville, TN 37214

Tyndale House Publishers
336 Gundersen Drive
Wheaton, IL 60187

UAHC (Union of American
Hebrew Congregations)
838 Fifth Avenue
New York, NY 10021

United Church Press
132 West 31st Street
New York, NY 10001

Victor Books
P.O. Box 1825
Wheaton, IL 60187

Walker & Company
720 Fifth Avenue
New York, NY 10019

Warner Press
Box 2499
Anderson, IN 46011

Westminster Press
925 Chestnut Street
Philadelphia, PA 19107

H. W. Wilson Company
950 University Avenue
Bronx, NY 10452

Winston-Seabury Press
430 Oak Grove
Minneapolis, MN 55403

Word, Inc.
4800 West Waco Drive
Waco, TX 76796

Zondervan Corporation
1415 Lake Drive SE
Grand Rapids, MI 49506